222

The Storm Collection

Tempestt Lyles

ISBN (Paperback): 978-1-963743-57-9

A Letter: Goodbye 20s Hello 30s

Well, I guess I'll start at the beginning. I was in my second year of college at Thomas University. I was studying Criminal Justice. I planned to graduate, take the LSAT, and attend Law School. But that is not how life worked out. I had an opportunity to leave Thomasville but there were other plans. I got into my first relationship with a friend. Where I should have stayed his friend but we were hard-headed. Being that he was my first he kind of had my head gone. He even proposed to me but of course, life happened. He was a cheater and abusive. But some days were better than others. He had me fooled and my pride would not allow me to go back to my family. Then, when he choked me unconscious I moved in with my aunt and we were going to work through our problems. Which was not a good idea because, in the midst of it, I walked in on him and a girl having raw sex. It was the biggest slap in the face besides him deliberately talking bad about his coworker and then marrying her. But karma does what she does best and that's healed and dead but it messed up my trust. Then I graduated from college and moved to Orlando. So that put me at 22.

I ended up getting into another relationship and that one was wild. It was all a facade. I guess I was feeling not fully healed. I wasn't able to fully be with him. But even though I knew that, I still wanted to pursue the relationship. I thought it was love but it wasn't just as the first relationship. This was my second relationship in my twenties. I was so confused because I wanted everything.

I wanted to be a lawyer, get married, and have kids. Living on a ranch being financially free and not having to take life on by itself. I was desperate, I wanted to get back into college and finish my degree. But it didn't work out like that. We went from different hotels and stayed in an apartment. Neither one of us was happy but we had each other and we thought that was enough. Being from a small-town family is more important but it wasn't a family we were having or trying to start. We both weren't sure where we wanted to be and it was like we were holding each other back. I knew that and I still held on but then in the second year of our relationship, he started cheating.

Now, at 24, I hadn't even started to go back to school. I was working here and there, the math wasn't mathing for either one of us. So it became a finical relationship. Still sticking together but he was cheating. I was fed up by 25. But then COVID happened and I just wanted him to go but pay the rent that month and stay with who he had been cheating with. We talked and guess what, he told me he got a new apartment and he would be leaving and he'll give me half the rent and pay the light bill. But he didn't and I had to figure it out because I just had to be independent. I didn't ask or tell my family about what was going on because I was still embarrassed about my first relationship so I had to do what I needed to.

Then I was 26 and it had been a few good months, he'd been gone but was still popping up and watching me from a distance and coming to my place and calling the police on me. He even tried to intimidate me with a gun but he wasn't the first. My first ex did the same and had me scared to leave so, this wasn't new but I wasn't afraid this time, I somehow managed to push him out of my place and it was a lot. So, when he started watching me and popping up I would always have protection there. But it was not cool because they didn't know what was going on and I was too embarrassed to tell my protection what was going on and I ended up falling. I just never felt that way before.

At 26, I was finally single, for real. I went crazy and started working a new job and really started loving doing electrical work and I had to deal with a breakup. I was emotionally drained. I was working with a man who cornered me and grabbed my breast. I started to think back and I saw three familiar faces. I was so sad and couldn't verbally say how I was feeling. I was just mad with rage. It was "fuck everyone." I was mad at my family because I felt like I was never protected and they didn't do what I needed for my sexual trauma. But they didn't know what was going on with me. I never told them what my cousins did. I only told them what the neighbors did because of the reaction I got as a little girl, I chose to carry the secret and only told one person.

I feel I am to blame. I didn't tell anybody anything because I felt like a child. When I told what Nard did to me I felt as if I was getting disciplined. So, I never told on my two cousins. But when the guy touched me at work, although I had asked him not to, I was still disciplined, D&S Electric Tech fired me and the reason was "I had too much going on." Everything that came out of the black hole, all those feelings came out. Anger was the biggest feeling that came out.

After talking with my aunt I started to feel better about being honest. It really helped with my addiction but the damage had already been done. I lost someone that I really cared for and it would never be the same. We still talk but I know it will never be the same and I am not mad nor upset, it's just I have to identify my pain and heal because I know no one can read my mind and when I started the blood pressure medication I knew I needed to calm down.

So, after I got fired from my job I joined the electrical union. I needed organization in my life, I felt like nothing was working and was convinced all men are perverts. Though not all men are the same, there are pervs everywhere. I learned no matter where you go to work it's always going to be something. Nothing is perfect. I'm not sure why I have had to experience these growing pains but they are there. I just want to live my life. As long as I keep my anxiety down and stop being triggered, I will be okay.

By 28-29, my anxiety was all over the place. I was very depressed and was getting triggered by everything. I felt like I wasn't where I wanted to be and I kept asking "Why me?" But I guess "Why not me?" I can't be getting stressed and sad about things that are out of my control. I need to be patient. It's hard but if I want to be successful I have to be. I can't keep letting haters get my attention and I can't let others try to get in my head. I need tough skin and I decided this earlier in the year. The same dude that did that to me that woke everything up was at my job and he was the material and PPE handler. I had to see this man's face every day but I had to put my big girl pants on because I had just seen one of the dudes that sexually hurt me at my grandma's house and the other one in close proximity to me and I lost it. So, the beginning of the year was a lot. I saw 3/4 people that sexually hurt me and I couldn't even do anything but just be there.

My cousin drove off to my grandma's house so I didn't have to experience him. But that same weekend I was starting a new job and I saw this man who cornered me in 2020 and touched my breast. I felt attacked, I told my director because in my head I wanted revenge on all of them. But I didn't know what I was going to do, like seriously. I told him I was okay and he was there for me but "I'm not the same Tempestt from back then." I'm not a victim, if you try me and disrespect me I will protect myself. I am not looking for protection anymore. I feel I am stronger but I am human as well. The shit hurts and sometimes it makes me rage and I have attacks, I'm easily triggered but I have identified the problem. Learning me was the end of my 20s. I feel like a lot could have gone differently but I am blessed to be alive so I say Goodbye 20s, you were the victim. Hello 30s, I am not the victim. I must be strong and I must stay focused. To learn me and to love me was the best thing I could have done. I no longer care to be wanted by people that I want to want me and that's family, friends, anybody.

30s are more about protecting my peace and getting back right mentally, physically, and emotionally. I love who loves me. If you lost me, that's your loss! Until the next book. I am ready to take on my 30s. I will not let it bother me no more.

Table of Contents

Chapter 1: Forgiveness Part 1

"Good Job," "Nice Work" are all I hear. No help is given because I guess I got it. Trying so hard not to mess up and that is exactly what happens. At my first job, I was being harassed and when I told the supervisor, he did nothing. The guy waited until one day when I would be alone. It was a fear he would try to do something to me so I tried to stay in daylight. I was finishing a room and I looked up to see my harasser. He grabbed my breast, laughed, and then walked off. I felt so violated. The supervisor had gone to the store and there was no one around but the foreman. I told the foreman what happened and he told me to call the police. To make a long story short, I lost my job and the reason was, "They didn't want to deal with my problems." So, I thought maybe I was the problem. I left the job with no argument.

At this time I had a boyfriend who I wanted to tell but he wouldn't believe me and he had the nerve to say that's what I wanted. Our relationship didn't last but 5 years. After losing my job because of this and my boyfriend's reaction, both hurt. Instead of telling him how I felt, I let our relationship run to the ground. I didn't trust him and he knew it. Without trust, it's only destruction. I tried to trust him but I went through his phone and that made our relationship even worse. We went on a break but that only opened more doors to our relationship that were left unclosed. So, there were all these people when it was only supposed to be him and I. Well, again I let it ride because we were together and I wasn't alone. Which only put me in a worse situation because I really started disliking him. But I stayed, he stayed, and we were together. After so many ups and downs he finally left but we would still talk. At times we would see each other but it only led to us fighting and arguing. We really weren't good for each other. We thought it was love but it was only lust.

Going through all these changes made me not want to work in the construction field anymore because of the perverts that worked there. But I couldn't let that stop me from working. Then, I worked for another company close to where I was staying. I could have lunch at home and after work I went straight home. I decided to be nice. But my niceness was taken as a weakness. I got into an altercation with a girl from work. She had been bothering me but I knew she was just a bully. I ignored her but that wasn't good enough. She keyed my car, threw food on my car, and flattened my tires. She was big mad at me. Now ask me what I did to her. It was nothing, she just didn't like me because she was the first girl, the only girl and then I came. I tried to be nice even though she was mean. It never worked and then she followed me around my building one day and she started with me once again. But this time it was awful; she had her mom with her and they teamed against me. I was dealing with the same problem. I took some time off from the job and then everything was going great until there was a change of leadership which led to even more turmoil.

I identified racism at the workplace and was fired. So yeah that's two times when I did the right thing and I was the problem. The third time I was a problem when a dude from work asked me on a date. I said, "Let's finish pulling this jet line." At this point, he knew I was ignoring him. He asked again but this time it was time for training. I got saved by training and after training there was a dinner for all the workers. So, I didn't have to deal with him directly. He saw me at the dinner and told me that he would be calling me. I asked, "Why?" He then walked off! Now, at this time, they were giving away gifts so everyone needed to be at attention. Fast forward to the time to leave, I parked on-site so I could easily get out. I left work and not even an hour later he was calling me. I know y'all saying, "How he got your number?" Well, we were working together and in construction, it's a big place and that's how we keep in contact. We don't have walkie-talkies or work phones, well, only the supervisors and some foremen do. After work, we don't contact each other. But, back to the story. I picked up the phone and was like, "Why are you calling me?" He replied, "What do you want to eat?" I said, "Nothing." He hung up and then kept calling me back.

Fast forward to Monday morning and I wasn't even thinking about him. But the foreman put us together to work. I asked if I could not work with him. He laughed and still put us together. I was working but as I was bending a 1-inch pipe, he was hating the whole time. That's how I knew it was going to be a long day. So, after he talked down on me, I told him I was going to the restroom, hopeful that all that negative energy was gone. After coming back, he was smiling, so I knew in my head everything would be normal. He demanded me to pick up something he intentionally dropped in front of him and I said, "No!" At this point, I was feeling extremely uncomfortable. I felt like he was trying to show me whose boss. He picked up his phone and called the foreman and lied and said I wasn't working. Instead of seeing what was going on, he split us up. Time went by and the guy was making efforts to come by to say something to me. I ignored him until he said he would push me down, we were maybe 50 feet on the mezzanine floor. I quickly called the foreman. He deadass looked at me and said, "If it's anyone leaving it will be you, not him." I felt really bad after that. I said to myself, "Maybe I am the problem."

They arranged for me to be moved to the night shift. They said that they handled everything but it was swept under the rug. They moved him to the night shift. I left work because I didn't want to go through it with him again. I ended up coming back because they got rid of him on my shift. I came back but I had already been talking to HR about what happened but they were unaware, they wanted to know why I waited. But I didn't, I had told the supervisor and foreman and they told their boss.

Long story short, they had neglected it. They didn't get in trouble, instead, one stayed on-site doing the same tasks while the other one left for another job site. Being there was the worst, everyone was talking about me, saying jokes and whatnot. One even told me, "No one likes you here, you got enemies everywhere out here." Well, I did and they fired me as well and blamed it on production and said because I didn't have any PPE on. But that was not true, I had proof but neither HR nor the bosses wanted to hear me. I wanted to fight for my rights and other women and I pray this book will get far to bringing awareness. I forgive everything that was done to me because if I keep finding myself in sorrow about what happened I don't think I will be mentally fit for anything. I forgive and I pray that change will come. But, at the end of the day, I have to be okay.

Chapter 2: Forgiveness Part 2

While I'm healing, I want to be forgiven, and I would like to give forgiveness. No, I am not always right but I apologize for any wrong or unintentional hurt that I have given. I also forgive those who have unknowingly wronged me. Because sometimes I don't speak out. Which would have me looking crazy, leaving the person unknown. Sometimes I feel that growth is not in everyone and everyone is also raised differently. So what may be wrong for me will be right for the next person. Understanding people should be first. But sometimes as humans that's where we are lacking. I cannot say I want to heal and I'm still holding on not forgiving anyone. Unintentional hurt, in my opinion, hurts the most because people don't know what they are doing to hurt you and they continue. They continue because it's a chain of experiences they are going through and the chains must be broken. However, not everyone is willing to break the chains. Instead, they pick another direction. Some may consider this as walking away. Which is good but, is it really?

Carrying hurt because you want something to be done and over is not okay! As well as holding on to something that cannot be changed. Being hurt only hurts you. Not healing after hurt can only cause more turmoil in your life. It actually starts affecting you. It's physical, mental, and emotional pain that can drive you crazy. It's an emotional roller coaster, it has no controls, and it's hard to tame something out of control. It makes you lash out at people.

It also makes you think everyone is against you and all odds are on you losing. But, that's really all in your head. Just because it didn't work out or goes as planned doesn't mean you have to give up on a situation. Some things cannot be discussed and you have to give things time. Although time sometimes is not on your side you must blossom and thrive. All the time you have to worry about yourself especially when it's affecting the way you are doing things. Forgiveness is big and it takes a lot to forgive and ask to be forgiven. Although they are just words, it's the actions that must be followed behind. What goes up must go down. I'm not saying it's all figured out but I will prevail!

Chapter 3: Practice

It's hard doing right when everything you feel is going bad. But I have to want to be a better person in order to change my situation. I can't be focused on what others do. I can only focus on myself. So, it's time that I do me. I can't rage every time something is not going my way. I have to remember that the devil is busy and when I'm thriving and wanting more that is when he is going to bother me the most. The devil comes in many forms. One could be as your "friend".

Even when I feel I'm being used I must learn how to control myself and not the situation. But I have to be able to control myself in a way that benefits me. For my mental health, I have to be strong and overcome all obstacles that may come my way. I know it's not going to be easy but I will continue to thrive and try to be a better person. I'm only doing this for me. It's been needed for some time. As I practice, times keep getting challenging. It starts spreading out at work. Although evil surrounds me I practice to do the best that I can. I was working on practicing the change but still, it wasn't good enough. I can't make everyone accept me and knowing how some people are you can't change them. I have to practice not to care what people say and do. Because they are going to do whatever pleases them. I must do what is best for me. I have to accept that feeling. I must go on because I can't make changes to anyone but myself. That's why I must practice. I have some resentment because of the things I have been through, which makes it worse. I feel like I must do what's right because it makes me feel better. Even when I'm not wrong in a situation I have to be okay with people not wanting to know my side of a story. Sometimes it bothers me and I feel like I must tell my side because I feel like I am getting hung. Then the lonesome and rejection feelings I have grow and it makes me sad. I get into a rush to go home and be alone. But I'm practicing not running away.

That comes with time although I'm doing good it triggers me and I just want to go into a black hole and be alone. That's why I'm trying to find balance. I must reward myself even if I have done the best I can do and it's still not enough to satisfy others. I can only do the best I can. I can't keep having anxiety over thoughts or something someone has said but it's all practice and one day I will be a professional and won't let anything bother me.

Chapter 4: Grief

I can't let it control me. I know it is okay to cry but I must not dwell in it too long. Grief can make you extremely fragile. I have to identify the grief sometimes. Sometimes you may not know what is wrong with you but you are hurting. I was young when I started dealing with grief. My uncle, the one babysitter I had was taken early, which left me in the hands of a neighbor. I got close to her and she passed.

Then, my grandma's death was hidden from me, she was my partner who I watched wrestling with. The lady whose purse had endless supplies of change that I used to go to the candy lady. I was hurt the way I found out and it has bothered me all my life and I was a child experiencing that. My aunt who spoiled me the most died. It was 2015, I was going grocery shopping so I went to my auntie's house. Whenever I was short on anything, this was who I turned to. The one that knows my darkest secrets, the one who knows me, and I am Tempestt around her. She was gone. I felt like something was ripped out of my chest and there was nothing I could do about it, the plug was pulled. I was upset about it and when I was grieving in the room, all they could do was try to make me leave. It was hurtful for someone to make a decision and not feel how I felt. It was hurtful and painful, I felt neglected but it wasn't about me. I just had to deal with it. It was killing me daily to know I had to share something that was mine because she was someone else's mother. I gave it up knowing she saw what was going on. I had to live on.

Then the death of my brother took me for a loop. It was hard, I couldn't manage the pain. I started being alone, it was like that blackhole was pulling me closer and all I could say was, "Okay." But then I got up and started working again, and then I tested every job as if I was supposed to deal with all the pain that I was going through. When I think about my brother I think about love. It's like a piece of my heart left me. I could not manage or control myself. I got weak and began to cry. The depression came back, then anxiety kicked in, and say what you have to say about your future, it's a slump and it becomes extremely miserable. When my brother died, it was bad for me, it was like an obstacle I had to push through. Losing your brother really bothers you in a way where everything is bothered around you. But there's nothing you can do about it.

Grief is real but it's something that I shouldn't dwell in. Thoughts come to mind many sleepless nights. It makes you mean in a way that no one wants to even be around you and then when you hear it from another person it's like they stabbed you and they go on but you feel like shit and it's not cool. You never know what someone has been through, know someone's background, or how something can trigger you until it's done. Sometimes the person doesn't know but it leaves a number on you. I know now that they are in a better place and they don't have to worry or stress anymore. With that, I calm myself but it still hurts. Grieving is a process that can take however long you need. But it can be controlled by keeping busy and not dwelling. It's more of a practice thing that can only grow you.

No one wants to be around sad Sally all day, period. People can feel that energy and it's not healthy for you or them because you don't know what a person has going on deep down inside. I try not to show my grief but I'm so used to getting bad news and feeling I haven't done enough, it's starting to show. Some people prey on that feeling and they know it. Some are just jealous and want to see me down. I will never forget my loved ones but I must let them go because it's beginning to get heavy and I'm not strong enough to handle it. So, I let it go, I will just never forget but I must not even miss them because missing them makes me miss myself and I will prevail.

Chapter 5: Love and Lust

We all know there is a thin line between love and lust but they are neck and neck. Dealing with a lot and going through different emotions can trigger both. Love is unconditional and that's the way I want to be loved so that's how I love unconditionally. If someone can deal with you and be patient while going through a healing process that's love. Not giving up on you when you and them know it has been a lot but y'all are hanging in there. So many obstacles come in life and so many people come in and out of your life. If you truly love someone you want to give up on them or string them along. Many people can say they love you but they go messing on the times you may need them the most. I'm not saying every time I feel sorrow I need you to hold my hand but at least be there sometimes. No one is perfect, people deal with a lot. There are a lot of things left unsaid and that's what can break the love. That's just platonic love if you are my friend and if you love me, show it.

I'm not hateful but I can be very much distant to a place I get and we may stop talking. I would want to reach out but because of the unsaid, I have to leave it alone because I don't want to be a bother. That doesn't mean I don't love you, I'm just trying to overcome hurt. I understand we are all busy and have a lot going on but we all make time for what we want to and because there is no effort, it's played off as being lustful. Lust is something to do. It comes with conditions. It has limits and I don't like it. If we love each other, let me know because I genuinely love people even if I don't like the way they are doing things. After all, that's just me. There is another thing people prey on especially if they can see a lack of love. Even within yourself, that's why you have to love yourself so you will know the difference. People will play until they can't no more. They will be with someone else and then back to you like nothing happened. But you get caught up in a fantasy where nothing really matters. Then you get a reality check and it makes you feel small where you have to pick yourself up. People say it's better to be alone so you don't have to worry about it but that's a lie! If we were meant to be alone we would not have to be together. But that's not how life is meant to be. You can't go through it alone and you need genuine people around you. However, people change so much that it's hard to come by real people. So, when you have real people around you, appreciate them. You will be able to see if they were sent by God or the Devil.

Chapter 6: Mood Swings

Sometimes I'm sad, happy, depressed, overwhelmed, mad, and upset. I am not only feeling this way to affect anyone. I get in my feelings just as well as anyone else. But I'm thriving and trying to push past all the heartache and pain. I will hurt sometimes and not be able to deal with it. Sometimes I say I want to be alone but that's not what it is, I just don't want to bother anyone and throw their energy off. If I'm sad I don't want anyone sad as well, it hurts me more and I would rather just go through the emotions by myself. I also have had people "there for me" but it was in their own interest, knowing there is something they want and need and I'm not trying to give it right now.

If I'm happy I love being around people. When I'm happy, I'm not sad, I'm not mad, I'm actually happy. I'll leave my house and be happy outside the door. If I'm depressed I'd rather be alone and sleep my way back to being happy. Sometimes I just need sleep and to stop overthinking a situation. I want to be around no one when I'm depressed. It's a sinking ship where I'll have you sleeping with the ceiling fans on. If I feel overwhelmed I just want to be alone because I don't need to lash out or rage at anyone. That could make matters worse and hard to deal with and could ruin any relationships.

If I'm mad, I'm stubborn there's no way to get to me. Unless you are that person who can get me out of the slump being mad. There's a name I can think of if I'm mad and when Elijah my cousin is around everything changes. If I'm upset I need to be around people that will uplift me and not tear me down. I would need to talk to an older crowd. I can think of my cousin Courtnee', she always knows the right thing to say to make me feel better. My cousin Razah will come through and she's the one that would most likely change my mood as well. They are comforting and I grew up with them. I know they understand me there's no discrepancy. The people I name all stay in different cities and states so it's hard. I have my Florida people that comfort me and know how to make me feel as a person when I feel like crap and that's a ray of sunshine.

Chapter 7: Exposure

I try to be around only positive people. People who motivate me and are truly genuine. People who are truly good examples to me. I have friends who are very fun and outgoing. But I have friends who are experienced and can show me different things. Show me investments, we talk about savings and real-life important things that can help me grow. I love growing and becoming more experienced in a lot of things. It helps me and sometimes gives me that extra push that I need to go on. I can push myself and pick myself up but it's good to know you're not alone in some things.

I remember my Auntie San used to always tell me, "You ain't the first and you ain't going to be the last. Fuck 'em!" I remember that a lot while going through stuff daily, it really helps me out and pulls me to myself. In life, everyone that is around might not have the same qualities as others but they are truly good people and 10/10. We grew up together and have been hanging since forever. I have two girls in Thomasville, Georgia, who are close to me and stay with me and make sure we talk. If my location goes off, one of them starts calling and texting.

When I think I don't have any friends she comes popping up and we have been friends since way back. They know me and sometimes we don't even have to talk it's the look and we read each other. We are very transparent and they tell it like it is especially the other one, she has no filter. It's fuck everything for her. She doesn't care, it's like she has no feelings but that lets me know she has more feelings and love than a lot of people. They are my girls, we are cool, and we have been through a lot but the friendship never changes. I cherish all my friends and I love all of them unconditionally. They all think I have favorites but I really and truly love all of them the same however they do deal with me differently. Some are more gentle than others but tough love is needed sometimes. It's not always going to be easy and sweet.

Chapter 8: What I Do To Ease My Mind

I do a lot to ease my mind and be able to go my way. Sometimes I play the situation out and I change what really happens. Because at this point it's done but it's not over. Sometimes I write in my journal and look at how sad and depressing it is and I make a better situation out of any bad situation. I make and sell products. I write books. I even go to work as a stress reliever but sometimes, most times, that's where all my stress comes from. I think I come up with a lot of different ideas and there are new things I can do. It takes my mind off reality but I have to get back to reality. It's hard, you can get lost and not want to go back.

I like to sleep to ease my mind. I dream a lot and most times when I dream I can see things before they happen. It's crazy that sometimes I tell people what I dream. I really don't have too many bad dreams, mostly normal-level dreams. When I dream I sometimes come up with a better outcome on what I am thinking about. I like to listen to rain sounds, it calms the room, and I am able to feel relaxed and can plan and think. I listen to meditation music and I tend to meditate a lot. I try to find a balance so I can be okay and if it's a rough day, I just change the day in my head and have a better outcome, that's me playing the situation out. I take long baths to sit and think of better ways that I can be. I'm always trying to improve myself especially when I notice maybe I am wrong. I don't claim to be right every time but I know I'm not wrong all the time. I have to ease my mind and have greater thoughts.

Sometimes easing my mind brings on a depression, so I can't be in the house for too long. I hate dwelling in my sorrows and beating myself up. But, if I do it, it will be hard for someone else to make me feel worse. I dress up and try to make the next day better than the day before and the best I can do is try.

Easing your mind is not healing, it's just a temporary fix that can only hold you for so long before all the thoughts start coming back. I have to forgive myself properly so that I can have my mind at ease. I hate built-up pressure when it can be avoided. I guess that's why I like to stay busy because it keeps me out of the way. Being out of the way makes some people nervous and they poke you to get a reaction. But instead of reacting I have to think and keep my head up. Because trouble really doesn't last always.

Chapter 9: Respect vs. Expect

I have respect because that's how I was raised. I'm still saying Yes/No Ma'am/Sir. No matter who you are. I would expect the same. But my expectations are too much because some people are disrespectful because of their positions. But that's not the way to be. I was always taught to treat the janitor like the CEO. That's words from my brother that never left me and will never leave me. Time and time people have yet to show me respect and I have given my most respect to them. But then there are still people who think like me and have respect. Just because you disrespect me I will not in favor give you the same energy. I will only be confused about why you have no respect. If you think you are better than me you are not, at the end of the day we are the same and there are no levels to this, you must act accordingly.

If you have disrespected me, understand, I am not quick to speak no matter what's your status in life. I expect people to be nice and have some manners. But people do not have manners and they would rather die than be nice. I can only take so much. So I try to stay away from disrespectful people. I don't like their energy, it's bad and it's not motivating at all. If I respect you enough to take your word I expect you to follow through. But not all, some people just say stuff to get you away and they don't mean what they say. But you shouldn't say nothing you don't mean just to say it. Although I expect respect I know it's not always given so I have to be prepared for the disrespect as well.

At the end of the day, people will be people and you have to stay true to yourself. Some will respect you some won't respect you but it's up to you how you will treat them. I can't count on my fingers how many times I have been disrespected and I let it ride because I try to be the bigger person. I will still be concerned about why people are the way they are but that's anxiety and it's too heavy. I can only be respectful of myself and understand people are not happy and some people try to make others unhappy because they are. If I'm unhappy I'm not trying to make no one feel disrespected, if anything, I'm covering up the pain and trying to make people feel good. I'd rather see someone smile when I'm feeling down versus making them feel shot because I feel that way. But everyone is not like me and I have to be okay and be ready for anything and stay true to myself. No matter what others do I will try not to let it cloud me. Sometimes I feel people when they are sad and when they are happy. It's not just them it's me too and I try not to carry others' feelings, however, I have to expect that I will feel them and have to be okay to prevail and keep having respect for others. Even when others come to me and tell me about the disrespect, I feel it, it's so heavy. I just wish respect was the only thing that humans knew, it would make the world a better place.

Chapter 10: Now That I Know, What Will I Do?

Now that I know I carry so much weight on me daily, I have to find balance. I can't run from my problems, I have to be okay. It's not easy but it's a process. I will prevail over anyone who stands against me and my journey, I want God to move them. I will be great and I will do great things. I will overcome all obstacles. I will find trust and won't be so quick to rule people out of my life. It's as if I will have no one in my life if I continue to block people because they are triggering me.

Everyone is not the same, I must understand that. Not everyone is out to get me, I have angels who surround me. When I'm feeling betrayed, I need to talk to a person and not just stop talking to them and they are confused. Because when people have done things to me I will just stop talking to you because they become a black cloud. Sometimes maybe the people didn't mean to hurt me but they did. I know I am sensitive sometimes and I could take things the wrong way. So I try to ask questions and get a better judgment. But when people reveal themselves to me I believe them. I know we all are raised different, so some people act how they were raised or become a product of their environment.

Before I cut anyone off I will let them know so there won't be any confusion. Some people text me and I don't have the energy to respond but I can't be that way. I will try to find a balance and get an understanding. My way of thinking can be different from anyone's way of thinking. I don't want everyone around me to be like me, I really want them to be better than me. I like to learn and I like growing and I cannot grow if I'm circling in the same thing. I will do better and be the best that I can be. I will try to communicate when I'm feeling a certain way to help me and others so we can be transparent and on the same page.

Sometimes I wonder if I am the problem. Am I normal? Are my expectations too high? I'm sure we all have problems, I will do my part, and hopefully, others do their part and we see each other as equals because no one is better than anyone. I will be a better Tempestt. I will only worry about what I can control and if I can't control it then it's out of my hands. I will not carry on more than I can handle. I know I can so I will.

Chapter 11: She Journey!

Right now I'm on the She Journey to become a licensed electrician. But, it's getting hard. I'm doing good in school but that's not all that I have to do. I have to work 8000 hours and I have to be on time. Right now I have 5000 hours but I imagine that time will go by faster. I'm in my second year now with less than 2 months before I get to my third year. But the closer I get the more problems come. People are truly making it hard. Being in a male-dominated world at work is crazy. First things first, not all men are the same. I have met some really good men. But some men make it hard to work. They want you to give up and quit and stay home or do a "woman's work" whatever that may be. But it only affects me when it's messing with my pockets. I have been fired for my appearances. Not because I don't have the right clothing or I'm coming in dirty but looking too good for work. I never thought I would be fired because I'm too prissy. But if you know me then you know I'm not prissy at all. I don't wear makeup at work but have been accused of wearing too much. Which was a lie! My eyebrows are extremely dark and thick and once I get them waxed they look good. They stand out. I wear eyelash extensions but no makeup. I have my hair done because I like my hair done. I don't get my nails done. But I do get my feet done. That's basic maintenance!

I feel horrible sometimes, I like to lift my spirits and it was my birthday that week. It was crazy how you get fired on your birthday. Some birthday gift! But that didn't stop anything though it had me depressed. A wise man once told me, "Tempestt, you can't let that bother you, people are just jealous. It's okay to look good at work. Don't let that bother you and you will start work Monday." I just kept playing it out in my head like, "This man is lying that I move too slow, while everyone else is limping and wobbling on the job site. That was just an excuse."

I prevailed and got over it. Through this journey, I never knew how hard it was going to be. But I forgave him and have moved on. I thank God for the direction He sent me in. I have met people who truly do care about me and my well-being. I find peace at my school. I met two mentors at school who really guided me. I'm truly thankful to them because this has been a rocky road.

Sometimes I like to go to school because it's comforting. I actually get a chance at school and it's really up to me to pass or fail. There's no jealousy, it's truly help, it's just a journey that I'm not giving up on. When I'm at work and the men say, "Women shouldn't do this type of work," it only fuels me because why not? I'm happy that the women before me paved the way but it's a lot of work. Women are tested in the construction world. I rather be in a union where everyone does their own thing. It's a long journey but it's all balance. I can't give up and I won't give up. Cheers to the next year and the following years that I may become a Journey Woman and a licensed Electrician. I love it when they ask me, "You think you're an Electrician?" Well, I am, and soon to become a Journey Woman Electrician!

I wanted closure from a lot of things but some things I will never get closure from. I must move on. As easy as it sounds, it's extremely difficult. Sometimes it's hard for me to let go but I must close all wounds and be okay with the decisions I have made. It is too heavy and not a good balance to my life and what I want out of it. The closure is to let it go. I know I will never forget but I'm letting it go. I will let life have my closure because everyone who has wronged me will have to find peace elsewhere. I don't have closure to offer to anyone, I just want everything from my past to stay in the past. If you don't like me for me just being me, may God bless you! I feel a weight has been lifted off my shoulders. When I write I believe that's when I'm getting the most closure. Because now it's off my chest and I don't have to worry about it.

Times get hard but life is what you make it. I can't dwell in my sorrow and be confused about others. I can only be myself. Others cannot have a hold on me. I have to let that and them go. Whatever that does not help me and only hinders me, has to go. People say they want closure but in life, they don't want closure they want to see how far they can go with you. I have to stand up for myself and protect myself, I have no time to waste. I'm focused on myself and how to better myself. If that's not enough closure, I really don't know what to tell you because I am done trying to please everyone and live up to their "standards". I have Standards and Expectations of my own. I can no longer take what people want to give me. Treat me right and I will treat you better. My closure is closed, I just want to be born again and I want a new life so I must clean this old life up so that I can strive and I will prevail.

Chapter 12: 222

Well, it's only right I give a 12th chapter. 2 plus 2 plus 2 equals 6. 6 times 2 equals 12. I give you 12 chapters. The reason why 222 is so significant is because lately, that's what I have been seeing everywhere. I always catch it either in the morning or noon. 222, I see it everywhere and the crazy part is I grew up on 222. That was my address, from childhood to now. I have moved but it still remains in the family. It was my grandmother's house. So many memories, good and bad. I love my family home when I'm home in Georgia, you know where to find me, 222.

I kept seeing the number 222 so I asked my cousin what does it mean when you keep seeing the same three numbers. She told me to find balance and align myself. I didn't know what that meant, I was so confused but I had to do some soul-searching. I needed to find myself, I needed to be balanced. I knew there were a lot of things that weren't aligned. I knew I needed to work on myself and become balanced. With the changes I was going through I couldn't balance myself because it was time for me to let go of all that I didn't need. It was difficult because the load I was carrying was heavy. I needed not only to forgive others but I needed to forgive myself as well.

I never knew I wasn't forgiving myself until I really looked into my life and realized I can't forgive because I didn't forgive myself. I had to forgive myself for holding on to trauma and talk to someone. I needed help. I was going through depression and I was not happy. There was so much weight on me that I started having chest pains. The doctor put me on blood pressure medicine. That's when I knew that was not what I needed in my life. I felt like I was too young to be on blood pressure medicine. I needed to let all the hurt go away and all the grief to leave me.

I am now off the blood pressure medicine and I manage my stress by letting it go. I can't allow anyone to make me upset. I must be in control of Tempestt. I can't let others have that power. I needed balance and I found a way to have it by letting go and not allowing it to control me. Or letting others control me. I had to put God first. I needed direction. I needed change. I had to be happy again. I wanted to be as happy as I once was. Before life got out of control. I wanted to remember my roots. I knew the people who kept me grounded were now gone. It was like I was living so freely but with so much rage and anger. It was hard to smile. There were some days I wish were over but I couldn't give up. I kept seeing 222. I had to wake up to direction. When you ask for something you must be ready to accept it. I had to get control of my life. I wasn't happy, I was mad, and I felt like I was being punished. I had no outlet. It was just me. I wasn't talking to nobody. I just wanted everyone to leave me alone because I thought in the end they would leave me or someone would turn them against me.

I forgave myself and now I'm trying to find balance and figuring out life. I'm not finished, yet, this is only the beginning. It will be a journey but as we know I will prevail. I am not alone and I have to be happy and live life.

Sneak Peek

Storm Diaries
Part 1

Chapter 9: Grand San

That's what her bonus granddaughter Milan calls her. She's my aunt as well, called San. She's the aunt who wants her flowers now because when "she's gone it won't do her no good." That's what she always says. She didn't bless us with any cousins but gave us unforgettable memories that my cousin and I share. She is the 9th sibling from my grandmother's side and the 19th on my grandfather's side. She's the aunt you will bother the most but when she bothers you, you are supposed to be okay with it. The aunt like no other, who flames up so quickly you can only love her.

Aunt San is very country; when she speaks you can hear it loudly. I remember on Teddy Street, Me, Razah, and Courtnee were chilling, using the WiFi. Razah left her cup unattended. Aunt San has severe OCD, she doesn't like nothing not cleaned and in order. She grabbed the cup and came to the door shouting at Razah. "Razah, dis youn?"

Razah replied, "Huh?"

Aunt San asked again all too quickly, "Is it Youn?"

Razah, still confused, asked, "Huh?"

Aunt San immediately slowed her speech, "Isss Thiisss Yourinn?"

I looked at Razah and said, "Is it yours?"

I lifted my head and told Aunt San, "No, no, it's not hers."

Shaking my head, it felt like I was a translator. The cool aunt, the aunt that you always end up being with. Sometimes it's like she's speaking another language but she has a heart of gold and she will literally do anything for her family, no matter how she feels.

She shows unconditional love but she's the aunt that will not say, "I love you." However, it's understood and the family knows she loves them, especially them babies, that's how she got the name Grand San. Milan loves her Grand San and we forever love our Auntie San; she wants her flowers while she is still living.

So, it's only right to take care of her.

Chapter 10: Through Drama Come Friends

I had a party where I invited all my friends and we stayed under one roof for one whole weekend. This one time a year was when I forgot all the drama and was able to see friends and family. I have a friend named Devon. He moved but he caught a flight to join the party. My friends Mari and Kiki also came from Ft. Lauderdale. My best friends, Brandisha, Khalil, Jaimee, Staci, and cousin Razah came from Thomasville. We enjoyed my birthday weekend yearly together. It is always a time to remember. I started to make my birthday party an annual weekend.

Over the years, I always walked around like nothing bothers me but I know now a lot bothers me. I always wanted to have a big birthday party with the ones I love. The same group returns yearly and we enjoy these times. Although it's just a house gathering we act as if something new is going on. We only want to see each other so we cherish our moments while we can and I am blessed that we can all come together at least once a year because we all have different lives going on.

I started it the year I met a guy named Sam. He was a lot to deal with. I used my first birthday party to get away from him that first year. It was a great party but soon I had to return to him. I didn't want to, we were at odds, and everyone could see it but there was no hiding. I did have friends to help me get through the pain. I'm not going to lie the party was everything but I never expected to lose a friend after the party. It hurt me because I didn't know what they were going through and they still showed up for me regardless.

I have had some good friends that I love but it hasn't been an easy walk. We all have our ups and downs but when it comes to being together, somehow, some way, we always manage to come together. Being my friend is hard, staying my friend may be even harder. I love them all and I wouldn't trade them for nothing in the world.

Chapter 25: I Have a Godson!

I wake up with a smile even if my day is bad because I have so much stuff to be blessed and thankful for. I have a lot of good people in my life and I would never want to hurt them or have them taken from me. Many people I have lost, some just left, and a few didn't have time for me so they didn't waste their energy. I rather you not be near me if I am taken for granted or no longer appreciated. Some people say I'm nice and it's often mistaken for weakness. So if I feel used I fall back completely. I'm not trying to hear your side because as long as I stay true to myself I can only expect others to do the same.

I treat people the way that I want to be treated, give love, and remain humble. At times people thought they would have so much over me but times have changed. I came to the conclusion that in order for me to want love or desire love, I must first love myself, and treat myself how I want to be treated, so there can never be any confusion if someone comes around. I must adapt and not be afraid to change, not everyone is out to hurt you but not everyone is out to help you either. Once you distinguish the difference then your world will be better. When I'm upset I find ways to not be upset as I look for the positive in things that will be great. I must not give up because my fight has only just started. I know when things turn around, I must wait, be patient, and not hold in what bothers me because that can have a lot of effects on me, then I lose control and the enemy wins.

My first real fast food job blessed me with a godson. I think about him a lot. Although I am not home, it's at a distance but that can only get better. I remember when he was first born, the cutest little boy I had seen. He came out with nice hair in small curls, a small little baby, wearing a Blue and Black Nike onesie. The experience was exciting. Picking him up and allowing myself to be there for his mom, I enjoyed being there.

Through different obstacles, I lost touch with my godson. Not one of my most proud moments. No excuses, so much was being thrown at me. I shut everyone completely out of my life. I became distant and very distracted to the point where I felt like I wasn't good enough to speak or talk to anyone. I used to spend my summers with the neighborhood kids, which all came to an end after moving to Orlando. There was so much on my mind and there were so many who I knew wanted to speak to me but because I wasn't available and I felt like I didn't have nothing to offer, I would stray away. Times will be better. I plan to be more involved. We will soon do an event together. I plan on giving my godson the world; when I make it, he will too! My heir, I will always love him.

Chapter 57: Jasmine…

My name could have been Jasmine, like the flower. Something delightful and joyful as heaven-sent. But there were so many Jasmines in the store that my mom thought it was a sign. My name ended up becoming Tempestt, often spelled Tempest, something like a storm. A raging storm was the definition that I was given as a child. What I was hearing caused me to bottle up and hold the Tempest inside, holding back the thoughts of Jasmine, a flower that blossoms. So, I held onto the name, maybe that was the change that affected me. Or maybe I was myself, Jasmine or Tempestt? I read somewhere that Jena meant Paradise, I guess that's where the Storm is held. Still in me but stored in a paradise. My last name was changed as well, I guess that's why I'm so big on change. I held on to that name. Playing sports, my name was Hulk.

Did everyone see me as a monster? Maybe not the aggressive energy that comes out. It was a rage that had no name. Thoughts that remain in my head. I guess my "Paradise" is stored so the rage is yet to be released. Smoky is a great adjective to describe the release. To inhale is to hold escape but for how long? Having doubts, mind wandering, never really finding balance. When balance comes the release is done and the hole is closed. It remains still on my mind but I overcame it. Now being able to speak and not holding things in is the best feeling. Having doubts, being unsure and unaware can only bring trouble. To believe it will get better, it will! I am my name, my name is not me.

Storm Diaries
Part 2

Chapter 60: Rejection vs Neglection

I already feel rejected by my dad. I don't like the feeling of rejection. Don't reject my kindness! Don't reject the way I was raised! Don't reject how I do something! Don't reject my understanding! Don't reject me! Don't reject my business! Don't reject my craft! Don't bother me if you feel you want to reject anything! Don't reject my perspective! Don't reject my efforts! Don't reject my feelings! Don't reject my hurt! Don't reject my fears! I'm human, I have feelings. I show tough feelings but inside I just want to explode. Rejection is a fear. Why is rejecting me so hurtful and hard to manage? Why can't I accept the love from a neighbor?

I opened up to a neighbor. She was nice to me but didn't want anything from me and she continued wanting me over her house. She was older than all the neighborhood kids. But she was the school teacher and we were her kids, hell, sometimes she was the momma. She always acted older than she was. She did the adult thing. I didn't like that because I knew I was going to get my ass whipped. I'd get in trouble when it was someone else's fault anyway. Well, that's how I feel when I know the situation. "Don't tell nobody!"

When I was younger my neighbor told my mom the secret. The secret I thought to keep was the wrong one to hold. My mom asked me what I did. "Tempestt, tell me or I'm going to beat your ass!"

My neighbor added, "Tell her so he can't do it no more." Not thinking that I showed my ass earlier, I was already in hot shit. This time with a louder voice, my mom asked again, "Tempestt, what happened?" My neighbor was looking at me, I was embarrassed. "He put his stuff in my mouth."

Fueled with anger and in tears, I blacked out. There are five times in my life when I blacked out. When it's too much I go into the dark room. But at that moment, I didn't want to tell nobody nothing else. So the dark room opened up as a child that stayed my safe place until adulthood. I had to put a lot in the dark room because had I told my mom about my cousins she might have whooped me or worse, made me feel like it was all my fault. I couldn't be rejected by my family and avoided answering questions. I kept that secret but my family knew about the neighbor, not just my cousin. I felt when I opened up that day nobody wanted me. I felt rejected, and I acted up to get attention but now I saw my cousins who I looked up to caring for another sexual abuse victim. I wasn't mad, I just wanted that love y'all, showed to a stranger.

Why I don't like rejection? I feel unwanted and unwelcome, and it reminds me of that scared little girl who was labeled bad as hell. My fear of being misunderstood builds up so much anxiety sometimes, I just sit and think because if I voice myself, I feel no one can handle it. Rejection is big, I keep my feelings inside because if someone I love rejects me, I cut them off. It's big for me. I don't like rejection and don't make me unwanted, that's another way to get rid of me. People wonder why I'm like this or that. People are for themselves. I care too much so before I let you hurt Tempestt again, I'll just leave. Maybe that's why I run away so much because I feel the rejection coming but before you reject me remember what rejection does and how it affects the person. This has been bothering me all my life. When I explained all this to my mom, she couldn't believe I remembered this. But we talked about it. I still think about it and distance myself from certain people but I'm trying. I'm really just working on myself. Being alone and free I tend to think a lot. My mind is all over the place and it shows. I try to piece myself together daily. I smile when I'm hurt. I hold my tears in but it's always the strong thing that bothers me the most. To understand me is to know me. Now it gets crazy when I have to reject something. Everything has reasoning.

Chapter 62: What Happened to That Pretty Smile?

I stopped showing my teeth in school pictures because I didn't feel happy. I held pain in from my childhood. I feel like when I was pure I was cute. To be sexually abused grows you up mentally. Some may even say, "Too smart for your own good." As a child, I listened more. More than you would think.

Staying at the house with my Uncle Popsi taught me at a young age how to cook and pick hair. But he left me early as well. It seemed like every time someone left me, the pain grew stronger. I never opened up to anyone because I always worried about how someone felt. Imagine feeling this pain as a child, or worse, nobody asking you how you are doing. Instead, they judge based on their thoughts. I was always called peaches, bad ass child. But, tell me this, what have you seen me do? Nothing, it's just word of mouth, stories made up, and opinions here and there. Or imagine you as a child being sexually abused and all you hear is shit talking but then you see your family basically adopt a victim of the same crime. Is it because I maybe talked too much or what really was it?

How can you judge me to say I influenced anything when you don't know me and to be honest, you never really understood me to know me. Why that big pretty smile left? You never even saw the change but for a stranger, you notice the unnoticed. I'm angry, I'm hurt, I'm bad as hell, I just want to be accepted. No need to smile, I'll just take the picture, it's not like you notice me anyway.

To be continued…

Family Bonus

Chapter 27: The Picture of the Little Girl in the Frame

I'll say one person who matched my love and understood me was Brandi. My first cousin Garret used to always tell me who my family was. My cousin Beatta didn't have any kids so I told her, "Put me down for an emergency contact, I'm all you've got." I loved messing with her. She didn't want you touching her, looking at her, or breathing around her. She didn't like germs. But I still go around her because she needs kids. Well, I would like for Beatta to have one. But to be around Lil Garret, David, Tyler, Quez, and Uncle Andre was everything. To hear Uncle Andre and Quez argue was hilarious. Quez wasn't putting up with nothing then and I know it's the same now, he ain't ever playing!

Then I met my cousins Kelley and Brandi and I'd usually call them over too. My Uncle Kevin and Auntie Peanut came to get me. That's where you get a full house effect from. Your mommy and daddy are there and they are both showering their love. Never did they ever make me feel like I wasn't theirs. Someone cooked in front of me for the first time with them. Experience is what you get being with them. Uncle Kevin, the cool uncle, he's going to keep it real. He's the reason I fry hotdogs and want them every time in SC. Aunt Peanut is his wife, she's cool too. She keeps your hair done, feeds you, and drops you off for summer programs. They are the same people. What you see is what you get. They are going to help you even when you don't know you are being helped.

Then there are Tyler's mom and dad. We ate out all summer and at times with them. My uncle really stepped up in a father role. I was convinced Tyler was my brother. Lil Garret, Dad, and Uncle Garret lived two doors down. We used to love going to his house but now he has moved so far away, I haven't seen him since I was a little girl. Then there is Teresa, Quez's mother, she also is my cousin but now Teresa and my bond has gotten stronger and closer. Teresa keeps putting me in my feelings because sometimes I feel she is not being sensitive enough though I can't ever have no attitude with her. I love Teresa to death and then on. She comes and picks me up from the airport, and I know Teresa loves me. It's just like being with Quez her son. I spend the most time with Teresa until she gets tired of me and I still call her thirty minutes after she drops me off. My Aunt Robin is a real auntie, she really does a lot without any acknowledgment. She has it stuck in my head now, "Be the lender, not the borrower." It means so much because my goal is to become financially free and I can learn a lot from my Aunt Robin. Her son is David, we are the same age. My Aunt Robin's kids are proper, nicely dressed, and fun to be around. The coolest and friendliest kids I know. She is my dad's only sister so it's only right we give Aunt Robin the most respect.

It's so funny, I see a lot of Aunt Robin in me and I don't even think she knows it. Everyone stays a distance from grandma so it's like you have to call everybody and make up an excuse to get everybody over there. "Teresa, grandma wants you to come over here."

Teresa loves my grandma like she's her mom. Me, Ridge, Lil Garret, and Uncle Andre were always there and there was never a dull moment. My cousin Marcus and Uncle Garret would come to get Ridge and take him golfing. That's how I met his daughter on the Fourth of July, I will never forget it. To this day, I go by my Aunt Red's house, then my Aunt Dot's house. "Hey, but where's Deizah?" The crazy part, both Deizah and Brandi named their baby Charlie. I remember the summers going to see my grandma and there was a little girl in the frame who I always saw.

"Andre's daughter," Lil Garret said. Uncle Andre is everyone's favorite uncle and to know he had a child, I worried my family to see her. I wondered why she was never at my grandma's house. Then finally after so long of aggravation my family gave me her number and my cousin Kelley's number. I called them both. Brandi talked to me and told me she would be over at grandma's and she came. She took me to the mall and I had fun. It was nice to be out of the house. To this day, I know the little girl in the frame is always there for me. It was like as soon as I came to South Carolina, Brandi had either just left Grandma's or had been there to see her. I could never get ahold of her but now we have our own bond and we stay in touch. Now Brandi has a little girl who often reminds me of the little girl in the frame.

Dedications

~ My Grandma Bet

~ Ridge

~ Courtnee'

~ Jordan

~ Razah

~ Jayah

~ Mari

~ Dee

~ Cousin Ashley

~ Jakobey

~ Michelle

~ Angel

~ Meshia

~ Pam

~ Karena

~ My Mom

~ My Aunties

~ All My Cousins

~ Nieces

~ Nephews

~ My God Son Kam

~ Mr. Bobby

~ My Sisters

~ My God Sisters

~ My Friends

~ L. O. M. L.

~ Mr. Bobby

~ Sean

~ Momma Dee

~ Anwar

A Special Memorial

~ My Grandma Mary

~ Ms. Catherine

~ My Aunt Maggie

~ My Auntie Sookie

~ My Granddaddies

~ My Aunt Courtney

~ Auntie Faye

~ Grandad J

~ Grandad E

~ My God Mother Dot

~ My Aunt Lady Bug

~ My Brother Jab

~ My Cousin Garrett

~ My Uncle Pop

~ My Uncle David

~ My Uncle Fat Tat

~ My Cousin Trent

~ My Aunt Dottie

~ Tricey

~ Lil Chris

~ Mr. Flowers

About the Author

I'm Tempestt Lyles. I love to write and create stories through my imagination. It's a way out of reality. I am from Thomasville, Georgia, and now I live in Orlando. I'm just trying to figure out life and I want to be at peace. I own Tempting Tempressed, Inc. Be sure to try my Tempting Lip Gloss and Temp-stick for your lips!